FUNDAMENTALS OF PRIVATE EQUITY FUNDING

SMALL AND LARGE-SCALE BUSINESSES AND REAL ESTATE INVESTORS

Solomon Lacy III

ISBN 979-8-89480-461-3

Table of Contents

Introduction

Welcome to the captivating realm of finance—a labyrinth of abundant opportunities and formidable challenges. In this intricate world, private lending isn't just a footnote; it's a pivotal force shaping the landscape of real estate. Drawing from my wealth of experiences and profound expertise, I, Solomon Lacy III, will guide you through the complex terrain of private lending and investment. With my guidance, you'll harness vast knowledge and understanding.

Many individuals hesitate to delve into real estate investment due to fear of the unknown. Some deplete their savings, convinced they need hefty capital for property down payments. Meanwhile, others are daunted by the prospect of seeking assistance beyond traditional lending, which often caters exclusively to well-qualified and financially affluent investors. Within these pages, I lay the groundwork necessary to finance and partner with you in real estate ventures, equipping you with the tools to embark on your journey.

I'm not merely a guide but a trailblazer—an enterprising CEO, seasoned entrepreneur, accomplished investor, published author, and Master of Real Estate and financial strategy. My journey from humble beginnings to commanding heights serves as inspiration and a pragmatic blueprint for anyone eager to leave their financial mark.

Suppose you're prepared to immerse yourself in the intricate world of financial strategies and navigate the twists and turns of private lending. In that case, you've chosen the right mentor. Let me, Solomon Lacy, demonstrate how it's done, providing insights only a top expert can offer while maintaining clarity, simplicity, and directness. Welcome to the adventure—turn the page and embark on your path to success.

Originally hailing from Flint, Michigan, and now a seasoned finance professional residing in Atlanta, Georgia, I have devoted over a decade to mastering finance and investment. My journey began in my twenties, transforming a boutique consumer credit restoration firm into SL3 Consulting, a consulting powerhouse in private equity finance. My profound understanding of the financial needs of individuals, families, and businesses globally has enabled me to provide sustainable financial solutions, raising over $120 million in Private Equity capital across diverse industries.

In 2019, recognizing a real estate lending market gap, I leveraged my extensive Private Equity contacts to establish a more advantageous hub for real estate lending clients. By negotiating superior rates, longer terms, and expedited processing times, I began funneling all hard money deals in-house to a dedicated fund, thus reshaping industry standards. My oversight of over $100 million in client assets acquisitions underscores my commitment to seamless and efficient transaction processes, spanning a spectrum of loans, including DSCR, portfolio loans, fix and flip, fix and hold, ground-up construction, multifamily, and commercial projects.

With features in esteemed publications like Yahoo Finance, LA Weekly, Entrepreneur, Forbes Magazine, and Thrive Global, SL3 Consulting has emerged as a go-to brokerage for high-net-worth clients and real estate investors worldwide. We specialize in facilitating connections, providing consultation, underwriting deals, and executing capital raises across industries, including cannabis, commodities, renewable energy, insurance, technology, and real estate.

My approach to closing the wealth gap revolves around providing access to information and resources beyond mere income considerations. Upholding the golden rule of prioritizing the client and delivering the best possible service is the cornerstone of my business philosophy. This book encapsulates that wisdom, offering readers an insider's perspective into the strategic maneuvers and decision-making processes that can elevate private lending into a potent tool for wealth creation.

How it all started

At 24, freshly graduated from graduate school with my first corporate position secured, I felt tremendous accomplishment. Yet, this high was quickly tempered by the realization of my inadequate financial planning.

Despite the external markers of success, my financial literacy was lacking—I hadn't practiced active credit monitoring or grasped the intricacies of financial health, leading to a precarious financial state.

This situation starkly contrasted my professional achievements, underscoring an educational gap. While I excelled academically, I had overlooked essential financial management. This oversight, a remnant of my "poor college student" days, taught me valuable lessons about the real measures of success—it's not about how you start, but how you finish. Eight years later, my perseverance and hard work paid off, culminating in a personal and business financial portfolio valued at over $5.4 million, a source of immense pride for someone from Flint.

Reflecting on my journey highlights a common theme many encounters: poor financial planning. Often rooted in a lack of information, upbringing, or misguided family decisions, making excuses is easy. However, we must move beyond them. As the saying goes, "Excuses are tools of the incompetent," especially in financial responsibility. We can't change our past, but we can learn from it to shape a better future.

Exposure and knowledge are crucial in making informed decisions. While educational achievements are celebrated, practical financial literacy often goes overlooked, particularly evident in the financial disparities within minority communities in America. It's vital to overcome the misconception that financial habits are predestined by one's background. With proper exposure and information, significant mindset shifts are possible.

For those reading who may have faced similar financial challenges, the actions you take now, armed with the right tools and knowledge, can dramatically change your life's trajectory and that of future generations. For me, embracing entrepreneurship wasn't just a career choice but a path to self-fulfillment. I am Solomon Lacy III, founder of Fresh Start Financials Group and now owner of SL3 Consulting, with e-commerce, real estate, healthcare, logistics, and authorship ventures.

My path was defined by societal expectations—earning a master's degree with honors, securing a high-paying corporate job, and fulfilling familial expectations through college football. Yet, despite these achievements, my lack of financial knowledge necessitated a co-signer due to poor financial planning, leaving me disillusioned.

The realization that I was no longer growing or feeling challenged in my corporate role spurred my entrepreneurial journey, born from fear, determination, and acknowledgment of my financial literacy and credit management gaps. My first venture wasn't Fresh Start Financials but an online marketing firm I managed from my cell phone while keeping my day job, honing my skills in social media marketing and building a global network of ambitious entrepreneurs.

People doubted my ability to overcome financial hurdles, but I proved them wrong. They said I couldn't secure business funding without a substantial business history, yet I succeeded quickly. Traditional markers of success, like degrees and corporate positions, weren't my ultimate goals.

I chose to leave my corporate job, humorously branding myself as "unemployed on purpose," and it turned out to be more successful than I could have imagined. When I stopped heeding the naysayers, my life began transforming—they were projecting their fears and limitations onto me.

Procrastination, described as "the arrogant assumption that God owes you another opportunity to do what you already had time to do," resonated with me and should inspire us all to be proactive and apply our knowledge. My ventures into real estate started with purchasing rental properties with my father in Flint, Michigan, highlighting how my businesses have resulted from exposure and skill acquisition.

This entrepreneurial journey often results in a significant cultural shift. One of the first things you notice is the emergence of a new following. When I first excitedly declared myself an entrepreneur to my younger brother, I didn't fully grasp what it entailed. Yet, I sensed the change in how others perceived and interacted with me, marking the beginning of a profound transformation.

Another significant transformation is the shift from being an employee to becoming a business owner. This change goes beyond a mere alteration in title; it fundamentally reshapes how you manage finances. In entrepreneurship, money is vital, and effective financial management often determines whether a business will succeed or fail.

The influence you wield in this new role cannot be underestimated. Suppose your product or service is high quality. In that case, your audience will likely become your advocates, effectively acting as a marketing team. One of the greatest compliments in business is a referral, signaling high trust. The typical business cycle involves people first liking you, then trusting you, and finally deciding to do business with you. How you operate your business is crucial to its long-term viability. My grasp of this dynamic deepened as I helped numerous families reach their financial goals, leading to word-of-mouth referrals that served as invaluable marketing tools during the early stages of my business.

I soon realized that my true passion was helping others achieve success. I seized every chance to interact with people, gather feedback, and create a positive atmosphere. Drawing on my experience as an athlete, I cultivated a determination to excel. Throughout my entrepreneurial journey, I adopted slogans like "WeWorkin" and "Wake Up and WIN" as daily affirmations. These mantras embody values such as diligence, a winning attitude, teamwork, dedication, and the commitment to exceed expectations.

Transitioning from an employee to a business owner, you'll notice a stark difference in how your efforts are rewarded. A saying resonates deeply: "You will forget the work, but the work won't forget you." As an employee, your daily labor directly contributes to someone else's business success. In return, you receive a steady paycheck. However, as a business owner, the fruits of your labor may not be immediately visible. It might take months or even years before you see tangible results. Business is essentially a numbers game—you face numerous rejections before finally achieving a sale. Each rejection should be a stepping stone; giving up too soon could mean missing out on potential success.

Those initial rejections are also instructive. The people who initially said no might continue to watch your progress and could become customers later. Perhaps they didn't need your product initially, or your approach didn't resonate with them then. Their eventual patronage underscores the truth that the effort you invest will ultimately pay off.

Entrepreneurship is undeniably a dynamic journey. You may come across elements of your business model that dissatisfy you. Still, you might lack the immediate knowledge to effect change. This underscores the importance of mentorship and coaching. In many fields, investing in a coach or mentor is a sound decision for any entrepreneur. The right mentor is crucial for both personal and professional growth. Seek someone experienced, knowledgeable, and who follows a successful system. Look for mentors who represent the business acumen and lifestyle you aspire to achieve. Cultivating a network of like-minded individuals—your success tribe—is essential for thriving as an entrepreneur.

This book dives into private equity funding, a vital resource for businesses needing financial backing. It aims to educate business owners on identifying projects requiring funding and navigating the complex terrain of private equity firms, which provide crucial funds and invest equity to boost liquidity. The range of projects benefiting from such funding is extensive, from real estate ventures to corporate mergers and acquisitions.

Over time, my career in the financial sector has evolved, leading me to specialize in business finance. After advancing beyond small business and personal finance, I have honed my expertise in the more intricate areas of business funding and growth strategies.

The core message of this book is to shed light on the transformative role of private equity in raising public awareness and reshaping the business landscape. It underscores the importance of accessing capital in today's competitive market, a critical factor for operating a successful business and managing substantial financial transactions. This book challenges traditional funding views, asserting that financial agility in business isn't just about maintaining cash reserves. Instead, it involves strategic maneuvering, often utilizing various negotiation tactics and financial instruments.

This publication also reflects on my experiences working closely with business owners, helping many navigate complex challenges, particularly managing teams of 10-15 employees. I've gained insights into identifying key business hurdles and formulating effective solutions. The book offers guidance and strategies for business owners to successfully navigate their financial journeys.

A deeper understanding of equity in a business context goes beyond its definition of representing a share of added value in a company. It signifies a more profound partnership than a straightforward loan agreement. When opting for equity investment, one isn't merely lending money with the expectation of repayment under specific terms; they are choosing to embark on the journey with you, investing significantly in the project's success. This investment can manifest in various forms, whether in a company, a product, or an asset class, and it involves adding value and ownership.

Equity is often misunderstood or undervalued. Many might prefer immediate monetary compensation over grasping the intricacies of equity and ownership. They may not fully understand the long-term potential of equity, such as residual income or the lifetime value of a deal, which could mean forgoing future earnings for a quick upfront payment, similar to the dilemma faced by lottery winners choosing between a lump sum and extended payouts. Statistically, those opting for extended payouts have better financial outcomes over time.

In my experience, particularly with what I term 'workpreneurs' – individuals who straddle employment and business ownership – there's been significant interest in creative financing. These individuals approached me seeking ways to secure significant credit lines or loans for their projects. Initially, my client base primarily consisted of such individuals, and my role often extended beyond financing to include mentorship. Through my mentors and experience in capital raises, I learned that lending isn't solely the purview of large institutions but can also involve consortia formed by individuals or groups to provide loans.

This realization about the nature of lending, especially in private-public partnerships and capital relationships, profoundly impacted how I serve clients. Understanding these dynamics is crucial in the financial world, especially when effectively supporting clients with unique financing needs.

Navigating the complexities of finance, especially in capital raising, initially seemed daunting. My initial exposure to this field revealed a multitude of unfamiliar regulations and processes. Despite this, my eagerness to be actively involved helped me close my first capital raise deal, igniting my desire to delve deeper into this sector. As I ventured further, I found people willing to trust me with underwriting deals. The arrangement was straightforward: I would find viable deals, and they would provide the necessary capital, with me overseeing the entire process. I obtained a financial manager certification to enhance my credibility and expertise in these discussions, a strategic move to align more closely with my professional pursuits and demonstrate my capability to source and manage client capital.

Refinancing multiple properties to reinvest in commercial real estate is a common strategy, although it requires significantly more capital. The essence of real estate investment is to leverage debt effectively. It's not merely about accumulating debt but about utilizing it to access more assets, which can lead to better investment strategies.

My role in working with individual investors starts with a thorough understanding of their goals and investment styles. Determining whether they are genuinely aligned with their stated investment type or are simply chasing what appears most lucrative is crucial. I can help them develop a more structured and effective investment plan by fully understanding their position and objectives.

For instance, an investor may have previously attempted fix-and-flip projects with significant personal investments, only to face unforeseen expenses and overextended budgets. In such cases, I recommend a more strategic approach. Rather than committing large amounts of cash to a single project, leveraging financing options can allow for diversification across multiple projects. This strategy minimizes risks and maximizes potential returns by not tying up all capital in one venture and reducing the likelihood of high carrying costs and potential losses due to project delays.

Understanding the nuances of real estate investment also involves recognizing the differences between residential and commercial investments. The choice between these depends on the investor's experience level, capital availability, and investment strategy. New investors often start with residential properties due to lower entry barriers. In contrast, more seasoned investors may opt for commercial real estate, which offers the potential for larger deals but also comes with greater risks and demands careful planning and risk management.

My expertise involves aligning various factors—securing capital, preparing necessary documentation, and liaising directly with lenders—to ensure a successful investment journey for my clients. Whether residential or commercial real estate, the focus is always on creating a tailored strategy that matches the investor's experience, capital availability, and long-term goals. This comprehensive approach to real estate investment helps mitigate risks and maximize returns for my clients.

The primary obstacle preventing people from qualifying for private equity loans is their financial history and experience. Key disqualifiers include events like bankruptcies or foreclosures within the last four years, which lenders view critically. However, it's not just these major financial incidents that can impede loan approval. Factors such as a credit score below 600 or incomplete application forms can also pose challenges. For those in real estate, having experience with flips or other relevant projects is crucial, as many lenders prefer working with seasoned investors.

The challenge extends beyond meeting lender requirements and includes effectively managing the project or loan. Lack of experience can be a significant barrier, as inexperienced borrowers may not fully grasp the complexities of managing large loans or projects. This gap in understanding can lead to rejections, as lenders are cautious about entrusting substantial funds to those who might not manage them appropriately.

Even minor missteps or disclosures can negatively impact applicants' chances during the application process. For example, mentioning a past foreclosure or financial difficulty during discussions with an underwriter can cast the applicant in a less favorable light. Moreover, the lending landscape has been complicated by unreliable lenders, particularly post-pandemic, where some have promised capital without actually having it available at closing.

This situation highlights why traditional banks, like Bank of America, often don't finance certain projects. The private equity sector exists to fill this gap. Banks typically avoid projects deemed too risky or unconventional, which is where private equity steps in. These private lenders are more willing to consider and finance unique projects that traditional banks might overlook, often engaging in serious discussions with business owners that traditional banks would not entertain.

Refinancing multiple properties to reinvest in commercial real estate is a common yet capital-intensive strategy. The key to success in real estate investment is the effective leveraging of debt. It's not just about accumulating debt but strategically using it to unlock access to more assets, paving the way for improved investment strategies.

In my work with individual investors, I start by deeply understanding their goals and investment styles. It's essential to ascertain whether they align with their declared investment intentions or pursue the most lucrative opportunities. With a clear grasp of their positions and objectives, I guide them in crafting a more structured and robust investment plan.

For example, investors who have ventured into fix-and-flip projects with substantial personal investment might encounter unexpected expenses and budget overruns. In such cases, I advocate a more strategic approach. Instead of pouring large sums into a single project, financing to diversify across multiple projects can reduce risks and enhance potential returns by not locking all capital in one venture, thereby minimizing potential losses and high carrying costs from project delays.

Understanding the subtleties of real estate investment also involves differentiating between residential and commercial investments. The decision often hinges on the investor's experience level, available capital, and strategic goals. Novice investors typically begin with residential properties due to their lower barriers to entry. In contrast, seasoned investors might target commercial real estate for its potential for larger transactions, which also requires meticulous planning and risk management due to higher stakes.

My expertise lies in aligning various factors—securing capital, preparing necessary documentation, and direct liaison with lenders—to ensure a fruitful investment journey for my clients. Whether dealing with residential or commercial properties, the focus is always on devising a customized strategy that aligns with the investor's experience, financial capacity, and long-term objectives. This comprehensive approach significantly mitigates risks and optimizes returns.

A primary barrier to securing private equity loans often lies in financial history and experience. Key disqualifiers such as recent bankruptcies or foreclosures are taken seriously by lenders. However, other factors like a credit score below 600 or incomplete application forms can hinder loan approval. Experience with flips or other relevant projects is vital for real estate investors, as many lenders prefer working with seasoned investors.

The challenge isn't only about meeting lender criteria and effectively managing the project or loan. Inexperience can be a significant obstacle, as novice borrowers may not comprehend the complexities involved in managing substantial loans or projects, leading to potential rejections from lenders wary of entrusting significant funds to those inadequately prepared.

Minor errors or disclosures during the application process can adversely affect an applicant's prospects. Mentioning past financial difficulties, such as a foreclosure, during discussions with an underwriter may cast the applicant in a less favorable light. Additionally, unreliable lenders have further complicated the lending landscape, especially post-pandemic, where some have promised funds unavailable at closing.

This underscores why traditional banks like Bank of America often shy away from financing certain projects. The private equity sector fills this gap, providing an alternative for projects traditional banks deem too risky or unconventional. Private lenders are more open to considering and financing unique projects overlooked by conventional banks, often engaging in meaningful discussions with business owners that traditional banks would not entertain.

The value of partnering with a broker or consultant in private equity cannot be emphasized enough. Many are reluctant to engage brokers and are concerned about the potential for additional costs. However, the opposite is often true. Operating without a broker can result in higher expenses and missed opportunities. A broker's expertise is crucial in securing the best rates and deals tailored to a client's needs, utilizing their extensive industry knowledge and understanding of the lending landscape. This expertise is critical in sidestepping pitfalls such as committing to a lender who fails to deliver, leaving businesses vulnerable.

The essence of private equity is mastering how to make financial products work to one's advantage. It's not merely about accumulating wealth but securing capital at the right time. This principle is fundamental to our approach and is the central theme of the book I plan to write. The book will guide readers through the complexities of navigating the private equity landscape, catering to those seeking financing for their projects or looking to enter the sector as brokers or lenders. It will explore the intricacies of securing funding, delineate the roles and responsibilities of various stakeholders in the private equity world, and outline the essential steps to becoming a successful broker or private lender. The aim is to demystify the private equity sector and offer practical insights for those wanting to leverage it for business growth or as a career path.

Understanding Private Equity

Private equity is a special club for investing in companies that are not sold on the regular stock market. Big investors, such as pension funds or wealthy groups, pool their money in a fund. This fund is managed by a team that picks out companies to invest in, aiming to spruce them up and sell them later for a profit.

Think of it as buying a fixer-upper house: the idea is to renovate it and sell it for more than you paid. These investment teams aren't just handing over cash but also getting involved in improving the company. This could mean helping the company grow, launch new products, tidy up its finances, or shake up its leadership team to make it more successful.

The people who manage these funds are like project leaders, and the investors are like silent partners, putting up the cash but letting the managers call the shots. They use strategies like buying companies with borrowed money to boost profits while aiming to improve the company's value by increasing sales, cutting costs, or expanding into new areas.

The goal is to make these companies more attractive to other buyers or investors down the line. However, how these funds operate has changed, moving from heavy borrowing to more careful financial planning. The level of borrowing can vary depending on how stable or risky the company is perceived to be.

Private equity is all about investing in different kinds of companies. This can mean stepping in to help a company get back on its feet, giving a hand to businesses that are having a tough time, or putting money into brand-new companies just starting out. Sometimes, these investors buy a big part of a company, which gives them a lot of say in how things are run. Other times, they might only invest a little bit of money for a small piece of the company, which doesn't give them much power to make decisions.

For really big investments, private equity investors often join forces. This way, they can share the risk so it's not all on one person or group. Working together also lets them pool their know-how and contacts, which can be handy for making even more deals in the future.

Growth Capital

Growth capital is money invested in fairly established companies that want to get bigger, change how they operate, move into new markets, or make big purchases without altering who owns the company. These businesses are doing well and making money but don't have enough cash for their big plans. This kind of investment usually doesn't give the investor full control over the company. Still, it does help it achieve significant milestones like opening new locations, boosting marketing, buying new equipment, or creating new products. The company's main owners might sell part of the business to reduce the financial risks. This way, they share the risk of growing with the investors and might use the new funds to improve the company's financial health, like paying off debt.

Venture Capital

Venture capital (VC) is a private equity investment that focuses on investing money into young, growing companies, often involving new technologies or innovative business models. These companies are usually in the early stages of development, from the beginning (seed or startup phase) to when they're starting to grow and expand. VC is especially important for companies too new to have a solid financial history or steady income and those that need a lot of money upfront, which they can't easily get through loans. Although venture capital is well-known for funding tech and biotech startups, it's not limited to these areas. It can include investments in traditional sectors as well. Investors are drawn to VC because of the potential for high returns despite these investments being riskier and sometimes offering lower returns than other private equity investments, like company buyouts.

Private Lending

Borrowing money from places other than regular banks and credit unions, like through private lenders, is becoming a popular choice, especially for people and businesses that have a hard time getting loans the usual way. This different way of getting a loan has a lot of benefits and is becoming more appealing to many. In the past, only banks had the power to lend money under strict rules, meaning you had to follow a bunch of steps and meet certain conditions to get a loan.

For instance, if a small business wants a loan from a bank, it has to pass several tests to show it's a good risk. One of the biggest things banks look at is your credit score, which tells them how well you've handled money in the past. A good score means you're likely to be careful with money, which makes banks more willing to lend to you. Banks also want to see a detailed business plan that lays out what the business wants to do and how it plans to make money, which helps the bank decide if the business can repay the loan.

Banks look closely at a business's finances, including reports showing how much money it makes, its expenses, and how much cash it has. These details help the bank figure out if the business can afford to take on a loan. Banks also usually ask for something valuable, like property or equipment, as collateral. The bank can take these assets if the business can't repay the loan.

The experience of the people running the business and how long it's been around are also important. Banks feel more comfortable lending to businesses that have been successful and are run by people who know what they're doing. The business's debt compared to its income and how long it's been in operation show the bank if it makes enough money to handle its debts. Finally, the type of business can affect the chance of getting a loan because some industries are considered riskier than others. Getting a loan from a bank means you have to prove that your business is in good shape financially, has a solid plan for the future, and is run by capable people. This is the reason private lending is quickly becoming a popular alternative to traditional lending from banks and credit unions.

When private lenders decide who to give loans to, they look at things differently than your typical bank. First, private lenders care about what you can offer as a backup if you can't repay the loan. This could be stuff like your house, business equipment, or anything valuable that your business owns. It's like saying, "If I can't give you the money back, you can take this thing of mine." They also want to see that you've invested money into whatever you're working on. It shows them that you're not just all talk; you believe in your project or business and are willing to risk your own money. Unlike banks that look at your credit score and financial statements, private lenders look at your entire plan. They want to understand what you're trying to do, how you plan to make money, and whether your idea will work. If you've got experience in what you're doing and you've been successful before, lenders see that as a good sign. It's like being good at a sport; teams will want you on their side if you've won games before. Lenders look closely at whether your business is currently making money and if it's likely to keep making money in the future. They need to ensure you'll have enough cash to pay them back. The reason behind the loan is also important. If you need the money to grow your business, like buying new equipment or expanding to a new location, that's a good thing in their eyes. Surprisingly, getting along with the lender and building trust can play a big role. It's like making a new friend willing to support your goals. Lastly, private lenders consider the overall situation — what's happening worldwide and your specific industry. If they think your business can succeed even with certain risks, they might be more open to loaning you.

So, in a nutshell, getting a loan from a private lender is about proving you're a safe bet, showing you're committed, having a solid plan, making money, and building a good relationship with them. If you can tick these boxes, you're on the right track to getting the funding you need.

One of the primary benefits of private lending is its flexibility regarding lending criteria. Traditional lenders often have strict criteria for credit scores, income verification, and loan purposes. In contrast, private lenders can offer more lenient requirements, making it easier for borrowers with less-than-perfect credit histories or unconventional income sources to qualify for a loan. This flexibility extends to the loan's purpose, with private lenders frequently accommodating a wider range of investment projects, including those not typically covered by traditional banks.

Another significant advantage of private lending is the speed with which transactions can be completed. Traditional lending institutions are bound by extensive regulatory requirements, leading to longer processing times for loan applications. Private lenders, on the other hand, are not subject to the same level of regulatory oversight, allowing them to expedite the approval process. This rapid turnaround can be crucial for borrowers looking to capitalize on time-sensitive opportunities, such as real estate investments or business acquisitions.

Private lending also stands out for its ability to offer customized loan structures. Unlike traditional loans, which often come with rigid terms and conditions, private loans can be tailored to meet the specific needs and circumstances of the borrower. This customization can include interest-only payments, balloon payments at the end of the loan term, and flexible repayment schedules. Such personalized structuring can significantly benefit borrowers with unique financial situations or projects that do not fit the standard loan mold.

Borrowers in the private lending space often benefit from a more direct and personal relationship with their lenders. This direct communication can lead to a better understanding of the borrower's needs and more collaborative problem-solving when challenges arise. In traditional lending, borrowers may navigate a complex and impersonal institution, making it harder to address issues or adjust terms mid-course.

Private lenders often specialize in niche markets, such as real estate flipping or small business startups, which traditional banks may deem too risky or outside their expertise. This specialization means borrowers operating in these niches can find financing and a partner familiar with their industry's specific challenges and opportunities.

Due to several key features, private lending is more favorable than traditional bank loans. It's often more flexible, allowing people with unconventional incomes or imperfect credit to borrow money more easily. These loans can be processed much faster, which is great for borrowers who need quick access to funds for opportunities that won't wait. Private lenders also offer personalized loan terms, which can be adjusted to fit the borrower's unique financial situation, unlike the one-size-fits-all approach of traditional banks.

Moreover, borrowers benefit from dealing directly with their lenders, making it easier to communicate and solve any issues that might arise. This direct relationship can be especially valuable in navigating the complexities of loan management and repayment. Private lending is particularly advantageous for those working in niche markets or with specific needs that don't align with the strict criteria of traditional banks, offering them not just funds but also industry-specific insights and support.

Private lending is when people or groups give out loans, but they're not banks or credit unions like we usually think of. This can include folks with a lot of money who want to invest it differently, companies that focus on giving out these kinds of loans, and websites that help people lend money to each other over the Internet. People with a lot of money might lend it out because they're looking for a chance to make more money than they would with regular investments. They can do this directly or by using a middleman. Companies that give out these loans usually focus on helping real estate folks or small businesses. Some online platforms let regular people lend money to others for all sorts of reasons without needing a bank to help set it up.

In private lending, you can find all kinds of loans, including personal loans for paying off debt or fixing up your house, real estate loans for buying or fixing properties, and business loans to help small or medium businesses grow or manage their day-to-day expenses. Personal loans usually don't need you to put up anything as security. In contrast, real estate loans might use the property you're buying as a promise in case you can't repay the loan. Business loans might need some assets from the business as security or even a personal promise to pay back the money.

One big plus of borrowing money this way is its flexibility. Private lenders can work out special deals that regular banks usually don't offer, like allowing you to pay interest for a while or having a big payment. They also tend to make decisions and hand over the money faster, which is great if you're in a hurry to grab an opportunity. Plus, for folks who might not have the easiest time getting a loan from a bank—maybe because their income isn't steady or their credit isn't perfect—private lending can be a way to get the funds they need. However, private lending comes with higher costs, including interest rates and fees that reflect the increased risk to the lender. The regulatory environment for private lending varies significantly by jurisdiction. It can be less stringent than for traditional banks, yet it still poses legal requirements that must be adhered to. Both lenders and borrowers must conduct thorough due diligence to mitigate risks, with lenders evaluating the borrower's creditworthiness and borrowers carefully reviewing loan terms.

The legal and regulatory framework governing private lending includes a mix of federal and state laws to ensure fair practices and protect both parties involved. Regulations may cover aspects such as licensing requirements for lenders, limits on interest rates, and mandatory disclosure of loan terms. Navigating these regulations requires knowledge and understanding to ensure compliance and avoid legal pitfalls.

In conclusion, private lending offers a valuable alternative to traditional financial institutions by providing flexibility, speed, and access to capital. However, the benefits come with associated risks and costs, along with a need for careful consideration of the legal and regulatory landscape. Both investors and borrowers should thoroughly understand the private lending sector to make informed decisions that align with their financial goals and legal obligations.

Private lending in Real Estate

Private lending in real estate is like getting a loan from a friend or a company that's not a bank to buy or fix up properties. Imagine you find a house you want to buy and flip (sell for a profit) or rent out, but you don't have all the cash you need. A bank might take too long or say no because the deal is too risky or because you're not what they're looking for in a borrower.

So, you go to a private lender instead. This could be someone with a lot of money looking for a good place to invest it or a company specializing in these loans. You tell them about the property and your plans for it. They're interested in how much the property is worth and what you can do with it because they'll take it as a backup plan if you can't pay them back.

Private lenders can be more flexible. They can work out a deal that fits what you need, like letting you pay just the interest for a while or making a big payment. They're usually quicker to say yes and give you the money, which is great if you need to move fast on a property deal. In simple terms, private lending in real estate is a way to get money quickly and with less hassle for buying and fixing up properties, especially when traditional banks might not help you out.

Why Private Lending in Real Estate?

Studying the dynamic world of real estate investing goes beyond just spotting great properties—it also requires having the right financial tools at your disposal. One such indispensable tool is hard money lending. Tailored specifically for the real estate investor market, hard money plays a pivotal role, especially when traditional funding doesn't fit.

Hard money lending offers a streamlined, asset-based financing route for investors eyeing quick turnarounds, such as those dealing in DSCR loans, fix and flip loans, and ground-up residential constructions. It's also crucial for those exploring multifamily dwellings or mixed-use properties requiring bridge loans and those needing full documentation commercial loans.

However, it's crucial to understand the limitations: hard money lenders typically cap their lending at $20 million. This ceiling means investors must look beyond hard money for larger endeavors—like major commercial projects or extensive ground-up commercial constructions. Here, the realms of private equity funds, private lenders, and networks of high-net-worth individuals come into play. These sources provide the substantial capital injections needed for bigger, bolder projects that hard money lenders usually avoid.

While hard money is a linchpin in many investment strategies, stepping up to larger scales demands a dive into deeper financial pools.

In the real estate market, there's a unique niche where private lenders and high-net-worth investors truly shine—handling deals that don't conform to the typical parameters set by hard money lenders. Most hard money lenders have a cap, usually limiting loans to properties with 1-12 units. Therefore, larger projects, such as those involving 30-100 units, often find themselves without hard money funding. This is where private lenders step in. They conduct thorough due diligence and decide to proceed with these larger deals because they have the expertise to assess risk on a grander scale and have the flexibility to use their funds.

Most hard money lenders are constrained as they are typically part of investment pools or lend out capital sourced from other investors. Spotting this gap, I positioned my firm to cater to hard-money clients transitioning to commercial projects that are beyond the reach of their usual funding sources. This strategic pivot addressed a significant market void. These clients, seasoned yet strapped for larger funding avenues, often struggle to secure finances for extensive group construction or major commercial renovations. Leveraging our unique position, we broker deals with funds, negotiating favorable splits and securing additional support despite being a smaller firm. Our edge lies in representing more qualified clients, which makes us an attractive partner for even larger capital providers.

Our firm also revolutionizes client engagement through digital marketing, disrupting traditional approaches. For instance, replacing the old model of hosting weekly events—which costs one client about $1,500 per event—with a 24-hour accessible webinar. This change alone skyrocketed their inquiries from 2-3 to 50-70 weekly, all within a monthly budget of $5,000. Many funds typically hesitate to collaborate with smaller firms due to concerns over experience and productivity. However, SL3 Consulting maintains its relevance and competitiveness in discussions with these capital providers by creating our own leverage, demonstrating that we can deliver exceptional value and results.

Loan Programs

Understanding Fix and Flip

This method of real estate investing involves purchasing distressed properties, renovating them, and then selling them for a profit. At the heart of fix-and-flip investing is the art of identification of properties ripe for transformation. Often characterized by neglect, disrepair, or outdated features, these properties allow investors to unlock their hidden value. For instance, a dilapidated house in a sought-after neighborhood might promise a lucrative return on investment once its interior is modernized, its systems upgraded, and its curb appeal revitalized.

The process of renovation is where the magic truly unfolds. Fix and flip investors must balance maximizing the property's appeal and managing costs effectively. From cosmetic upgrades like fresh paint and stylish fixtures to more substantial renovations such as kitchen remodels or structural repairs, every decision must be guided by a keen understanding of market demands and trends. For example, investing in energy-efficient upgrades or smart home technology can enhance the property's desirability and command a higher selling price in today's eco-conscious market.

Moreover, success in fix-and-flip investing hinges on dealing with the complexities of the real estate market with finesse. Thorough market analysis is indispensable, enabling investors to make informed decisions about pricing, timing, and target demographics. By staying attuned to local market trends, comparable sales data, and emerging neighborhood developments, investors can optimize their renovation plans to align with buyer preferences and maximize profitability.

A compelling example illustrates the intricate interplay of strategy and execution in fix-and-flip investing. Consider an investor who acquires a distressed property in a prime location for $150,000. After investing $50,000 in renovations, the property undergoes a stunning transformation, boasting modern amenities and impeccable design. With careful consideration of market dynamics, the investor lists the property for sale at $300,000, reflecting its enhanced value. Within a short period, a buyer recognizes the property's allure and acquires it for $280,000, yielding a net profit of $20,000 after accounting for selling costs and financing fees.

In principle, fix-and-flip investing embodies the convergence of entrepreneurship, skill, and financial savvy. It empowers investors to breathe new life into neglected properties, enriching communities and revitalizing neighborhoods. Through meticulous planning, strategic execution, and a deep understanding of market dynamics, investors can harness the transformative power of fix-and-flip endeavors to turn distressed properties into profitable assets, one renovation at a time.

Turn run-down properties into lucrative investments through Express Capital Financing's Fix and Flip loan initiative. Whether you aim to acquire a property needing repair, revamp a duplex, or convert a warehouse into a multifamily dwelling, we offer the necessary support to kickstart your project. Our Fix and Flip loan program boasts a straightforward application procedure and prompt underwriting, guaranteeing speedy access to funds precisely when you require them.

Ground-up Construction Loans

A ground-up construction loan is a financial product tailored to provide funding for developing a new construction project from inception to completion. Unlike traditional mortgages or loans for purchasing existing properties, ground-up construction loans are specifically designed to cover the costs of building a structure from scratch.

The process typically begins with the borrower, often a developer or investor, applying for a loan from a lender. This involves presenting detailed plans and specifications for the proposed construction project and information about the borrower's financial standing and experience in real estate development. Before approving the loan, the lender evaluates the project's feasibility, the borrower's creditworthiness, and other relevant factors.

Once approved, the lender disburses funds to the borrower in stages or "draws" as construction progresses.

These disbursements are usually based on the construction plan's predetermined milestones or completion stages. For instance, funds may be released for site preparation, foundation construction, framing, roofing, interior work, etc.

During the construction phase, the borrower typically pays interest only on the funds that have been disbursed, helping to minimize the financial burden. After construction is complete, the loan may convert to a traditional mortgage or another type of long-term financing, depending on the borrower's preferences and the lender's terms.

Ground-up construction loans are often secured by the built property and other borrower's assets. Lenders may also require personal guarantees from the borrower or other forms of collateral to mitigate the risk associated with financing a project that has yet to be completed.

Throughout construction, the lender may conduct periodic inspections to ensure the project proceeds according to plan, and the funds are used appropriately. This helps to protect the lender's interests and ensures that the project stays on track.

Overall, ground-up construction loans play a vital role in facilitating the development of new real estate projects, whether it's a single-family home, a multi-unit residential building, a commercial property, or a mixed-use development. By providing funding tailored to the specific needs of construction projects, these loans enable developers and investors to bring their visions to life and contribute to the growth and revitalization of communities.

Picture a construction loan that mirrors your flexibility and reliability. Our ground-up construction loans are meticulously crafted with a singular aim: to ensure your building project unfolds seamlessly and triumphantly. Through our Ground-Up Construction loan, you'll experience the advantages of a personalized loan without any downsides: no prepayment penalties, concealed fees, undisclosed costs—only unparalleled flexibility and steadfast reliability precisely when required.

DSCR Loans

A Debt Service Coverage Ratio (DSCR) loan is a financing arrangement commonly utilized in commercial real estate. It evaluates a property's capability to generate adequate income to cover its debt obligations, including mortgage payments. The DSCR is determined by dividing the property's Net Operating Income (NOI) by its annual debt service, expressing the result as a ratio.

Lenders often stipulate a minimum DSCR requirement for loan approval, which varies based on risk tolerance, property type, and market conditions. For example, a lender might demand a DSCR of 1.25, indicating that the property's NOI must be at least 1.25

times its debt service.

This metric serves as a crucial tool for lenders to assess risk. A higher DSCR implies greater cash flow stability and lower default risk, making the loan more appealing. Conversely, a lower DSCR suggests a higher risk of insufficient cash flow to meet debt obligations.

For example, an office building generates an NOI of $500,000 annually and has an annual debt service of $400,000. The DSCR would be calculated as $500,000 / $400,000 = 1.25. This indicates that the property's income exceeds its debt obligations by 1.25 times, meeting the lender's requirement if they specified a minimum DSCR of 1.25. or an Apartment complex with an NOI of $700,000 and an annual debt service of $600,000. The DSCR calculation would be $700,000 / $600,000 = 1.17. This means the property's income covers its debt obligations by 1.17 times. While this might meet some lenders' requirements, others might seek a higher DSCR.

A DSCR loan helps lenders assess if a property can generate enough income to cover its debts, aiding in smart lending decisions for commercial real estate. Choose our flexible DSCR loan for your real estate investments. It's customized to fit your properties and offers the best features of various loan types. Opt for our DSCR Portfolio loan to finance multiple properties. It allows you to invest in single-family homes, duplexes, condos, or townhomes tailored to your needs.

Bridge Loans for Multifamily and Mixed-Use Investments

Bridge loans for multifamily and mixed-use investments serve as short-term financing solutions that bridge the gap between property acquisition and permanent financing or sale. They are particularly beneficial for investors and developers seeking to acquire, renovate, or reposition multifamily or mixed-use properties.

Imagine a real estate investor eyeing a multifamily apartment complex or a mixed-use building featuring retail spaces and residential units. The investor spots an opportunity in a bustling urban area undergoing revitalization, where property values are anticipated to rise significantly. However, securing traditional financing for acquiring and renovating the property may pose challenges due to factors like its current state, market volatility, or the investor's credit history.

In such situations, bridge loans offer a viable solution. They provide the investor with funds to swiftly acquire the property, renovate or redevelop it to boost its value, and eventually refinance with long-term financing or sell the property for profit. Here's how bridge loans are used for multifamily and mixed-use investments. Investors utilize bridge loans to finance property acquisitions, enabling them to act promptly in competitive markets or seize attractive investment opportunities without waiting for traditional financing approval. An investor identifies a mixed-use property with retail spaces on the ground floor and residential units above. It is listed at an appealing price due to its condition and the seller's urgency. The investor secures a bridge loan to swiftly acquire the property and initiate renovations. Bridge loan funds are used to renovate, reposition, or upgrade the multifamily or mixed-use property, including amenities, curb appeal, residential units, or tenant quality.

After using a bridge loan to buy a worn-out apartment complex, the investor fixes up the units, upgrades kitchens, and bathrooms, and adds nice stuff like a gym to attract better tenants. Then, they decide what to do next. They might get a better loan for the property or sell it to make money from the improvements they made. In this case, they got a better loan after fixing things up. With the property worth more and bringing in more rent, it's a good long-term investment.

Bridge loans for apartments and mixed-use buildings allow investors and developers to act fast, buy properties, fix them, and make more money from their real estate investments.

Lite Doc Commercial Mortgage: Bank Statement Loans for Commercial Investors

A Lite Doc Commercial Mortgage, or Bank Statement Loans for Commercial Investors, is tailored for self-employed individuals or business owners with difficulty documenting income using traditional methods like tax returns or financial statements. These loans assess qualification based on bank statements, offering an alternative financing avenue for those with irregular income or non-traditional revenue sources.

Lite Doc loans require minimal documentation compared to traditional mortgages. Borrowers typically provide bank statements covering a specified period to demonstrate income and cash flow. Qualification focuses on bank statements and cash flow history, with lenders assessing average monthly deposits and reserves. Credit history and other factors are considered, but income shown in bank statements carries significant weight.

Instead of relying on tax returns, self-employed individuals or business owners can use bank statements as proof of income. This is advantageous for those with fluctuating or multiple revenue streams. Lite Doc Commercial Mortgages offer flexible terms, including adjustable interest rates and repayment periods, depending on factors like creditworthiness and property type. For example, a self-employed consultant's tax returns may not fully reflect their earnings due to deductions. With Lite Doc financing, they qualify based on accurate cash flow shown in bank statements. Another example would be a restaurant owner experiencing seasonal revenue fluctuations may struggle to qualify for traditional loans. Lite Doc financing considers their average monthly income over time, reflecting their business's viability.

Lite Doc Commercial Mortgages provides a flexible financing option for self-employed individuals and business owners with unconventional income documentation needs, enabling them to access commercial real estate financing more readily.

Full Doc Commercial Mortgage

A Full Doc Commercial Mortgage is a commercial loan requiring extensive documentation of the borrower's income, assets, and financial history. Unlike Lite Doc or No Doc loans, which have relaxed documentation requirements, Full Doc mortgages typically demand thorough paperwork to verify the borrower's ability to repay the loan. These loans offer borrowers a range of financing options tailored to their needs, making them an attractive choice for commercial real estate investors and business owners seeking comprehensive financing solutions.

Documentation Requirements: Full Doc Commercial Mortgages necessitate comprehensive documentation, including but not limited to tax returns, financial statements, bank statements, business income statements, and personal or business credit reports. Borrowers must provide evidence of their income, assets, liabilities, and credit history to qualify for the loan.

For example, a business owner interested in purchasing a commercial property submits their tax returns for the past two years, along with financial statements detailing their company's revenue, expenses, and profitability. Additionally, they provide personal and business bank statements to demonstrate cash flow and reserves.

The qualification process involves lenders evaluating the borrower's financial health, creditworthiness, and ability to repay the loan based on the documentation provided. They analyze debt-to-income ratio, credit score, business stability, and property cash flow to determine eligibility and loan terms.

An example could be a real estate investor applying for a Full Doc Commercial Mortgage to acquire an office building. The lender reviews the investor's tax returns, financial statements, and credit reports to assess their financial stability and repayment capacity. The investor qualifies for a competitive loan with favorable terms based on their strong credit history and healthy debt-to-income ratio.

Full Doc Commercial Mortgages financing options offer borrowers various options tailored to their needs and investment objectives. These may include fixed-rate or adjustable-rate loans, different amortization periods, and various loan-to-value (LTV) ratios to accommodate different property types and borrower profiles.

For example, a property developer seeks financing to construct a mixed-use development. With a Full Doc

Commercial Mortgage, they can choose between fixed-rate or adjustable-rate financing, depending on their risk tolerance and market conditions. They opt for a fixed-rate loan with a 25-year amortization period to lock in stable payments over the long term.

The type of Properties Full Doc Commercial Mortgages can finance a wide range of commercial properties, including office buildings, retail centers, industrial facilities, multifamily apartments, hotels, and mixed-use developments. Borrowers can select the loan structure best suits their investment goals and property type.

For example, a business owner may want to purchase an industrial warehouse for their expanding manufacturing operations. They apply for a Full Doc Commercial Mortgage to finance the acquisition. The lender offers a loan with favorable terms tailored to industrial properties, such as a higher LTV ratio and longer amortization period.

Full Doc Commercial Mortgage provides borrowers with unmatched financing flexibility and options, allowing them to choose the loan structure that best aligns with their financial situation, investment objectives, and property type. With thorough documentation requirements and rigorous qualification standards, these loans offer borrowers the confidence and assurance to secure financing for their commercial real estate ventures.

Typical Loans and Terms in Private Lending

The amount you can get from a private lender depends on what you need the money for, how much the lender trusts you, and what you're offering as security (like your house or another property). Sometimes, you can borrow a small amount, like a few thousand dollars, especially for personal loans. For bigger projects, like buying real estate or funding a business, you could look at loans that go into the hundreds of thousands or even more. Personal loans might have terms from 1 to 5 years, while real estate and business loans could have terms up to 15-30 years if they are more structured, though shorter terms are common in private lending.

Interest Rates: The interest rate is the cost of borrowing the money. Private loans usually have higher interest rates compared to traditional bank loans. This is because private lenders often take on more risk by lending to people or projects that banks might avoid. The exact rate can vary widely based on what you're borrowing the money for, how risky the lender thinks the loan is, and how long it'll take to pay it back.

Repayment Terms: This is about how long you have to repay the loan and what your payments look like. Private lending is pretty flexible here. You might have a short-term loan that you pay back in a year or less or a longer-term loan that stretches out over several years. Some loans might let you pay interest for a while, with the big payment (the principal) due at the end of the term. Others might require regular payments of interest and principal right from the start.

Security or Collateral: Many private lenders will ask for some kind of security for the loan, meaning something of value they can take if you don't pay back the loan. This could be the property you're buying with the loan or other assets you own. Offering collateral can sometimes help you get a better interest rate since it reduces the risk for the lender.

Fees: Besides interest, there might be additional costs for getting a private loan. These can include fees for setting up the loan, early repayment, or other charges. It's important to ask about these upfront so you're not surprised later on.

So when you get a loan from a private lender, the amount you can borrow, how much it'll cost you, how long you have to pay it back, and what you need to offer as security can all vary. It's a lot more flexible than bank loans, but it can also be more expensive because of the higher risk for the lender.

My Private Equity Structure

At SL3 Consulting, we redefine the traditional role of brokers, positioning ourselves as architects of opportunity and pioneers in capital connections. Our expertise extends beyond mere deal brokering—we design pathways for growth, engineer collaborative ventures, and navigate toward new possibilities. Our ability to forge strategic partnerships and capital relationships distinguishes us from others. Our extensive network, including warehouse line providers, family offices, venture capitalists, private equity funds, international hedge funds, and real estate investment trusts (REITs), is united by a shared goal to enhance our service efficiency for our clients.

SL3 Consulting is a beacon of influence in the industry, a dynamic force for transformation, and a powerful conduit for financial prosperity. Our vast and unparalleled global network allows us to handle complex negotiations with finesse. We leverage this network to influence critical decisions and generate significant impact. At SL3 Consulting, our approach to brokerage services is revolutionary. We are committed to building and maintaining the finest client relationships in the sector, driven by a legacy of excellence and a vision that reaches the future.

As your trusted partner, we are dedicated to guiding you through the intricacies of capital acquisition, facilitating international transactions, and pursuing lucrative investments. Our approach is about meeting and redefining expectations as we continue leading in the brokerage industry with exceptional service and forward-thinking strategies.

At SL3 Consulting, our methodology is built on a multifaceted foundation, each element contributing to a comprehensive and effective approach:

1. **Unrivaled Network:** Our expansive network is a web of global connections across continents, industries, and sectors. This vast network empowers us to build bridges and forge alliances in areas others may not even perceive, offering a unique competitive advantage.

2. **Strategic Vision:** Our team is adept at identifying emerging trends and potential opportunities. This strategic foresight informs every decision, ensuring our clients are consistently positioned ahead of the curve.

3. **Masterful Negotiation:** Negotiation is an art form we have meticulously refined. Our tactics are designed to secure favorable terms, lucrative agreements, and transformative partnerships, setting the stage for unparalleled success.

4. **Result-Driven Focus:** Our ethos is rooted in the tangible impacts we create. We are dedicated to delivering measurable success for our clients, driving them toward achievements previously unimagined.

5. **Trust and Integrity:** The cornerstone of our practice is our commitment to ethical conduct, transparency, and integrity. Clients entrust us with their interests, confident in

our professional and principled approach.

6. **Strategic Alliances:** Our extensive network includes industry specialists and financial experts, opening doors to myriad debt and equity opportunities aligned with our clients' financial goals.

7. **Tailored Guidance:** Recognizing the uniqueness of each business owner, our seasoned brokers take the time to understand individual goals, risk tolerance, and preferences, leading to bespoke investment strategies that resonate deeply with our client's visions.

8. **Global Reach:** Our international footprint and profound understanding of global markets enable us to offer diverse investment options, encouraging our clients to diversify across geographical and industry boundaries.

9. **Transparency and Trust:** Integrity is the bedrock of our operations. We commit to clear, honest communication, equipping our clients with the necessary information to make well-informed decisions.

10. **Cutting-Edge Technology:** Leveraging the latest in fintech, our platforms provide seamless monitoring, analysis, and execution of trades, putting our clients at the forefront of the financial world.

Market Insights: Our comprehensive market research and analysis give our clients a competitive edge, informing them of market trends, emerging opportunities, and potential risks, enabling them to navigate the complex investment landscape confidently and clearly.

How Beneficial is a Business Loan?

Engaging with a business loan can be a strategic move for growth-oriented companies, providing the necessary leverage to expand operations, enter new markets, or enhance existing capabilities. When managed wisely, a business loan can propel a company to new heights of success and profitability.

Capital Investments

Invest in essential equipment to improve your business operations and stimulate growth. This includes various tools and machinery, such as machine tools for manufacturing processes, heavy machinery for construction or industrial tasks, and specialized devices for medical or diagnostic purposes.

Employee Recruitment and Development

Invest in your workforce, your most valuable asset. Small business financing loans at low-interest rates enable you to recruit new talent and expand your business more feasibly.

Debt Consolidation

Simplify your business's financial commitments by consolidating multiple debts into a single monthly payment with a lower interest rate. This strategy streamlines your finances and often reduces interest costs, freeing up resources for daily operations.

Term Loans

Gain immediate funding to enhance, expand, or establish additional locations for your business. In regions like California, small business loans are known for their low-interest rates and swift approval processes, providing a quick financial boost to meet your business needs.

International Trade Financing

SL3 Consulting is a leader in trade finance consulting, distinguished by our expert facilitation of a diverse array of financial instruments. Our expertise spans local and international markets, ensuring global reach and comprehensive solutions for our clients.

Our commitment is steadfast in providing each client with the specific trade finance services they need, delivered efficiently and effectively. Our offerings include, but are not limited to, Standby Letters of Credit (SBLC), Bank Guarantees (BG), and Letters of Credit (LC) solutions. Each of these financial tools is crafted to provide security and facilitate smooth transactions in international trade.

However, our services extend beyond these instruments. We offer a complete suite of trade services to empower your business ventures. In an ever-evolving global economy, we aim to equip you with the financial tools and insights necessary for your business to thrive and succeed.

At SL3 Consulting, we see our role as more than just transactional interactions. We are committed to building lasting relationships with our clients and partners. Our journey with you is about establishing a partnership based on trust and mutual growth. We strive to be more than consultants; we aim to be your trusted allies, supporting you at every step of your business journey.

We understand the complexities of global trade and are dedicated to navigating these challenges with you. Our team of experts is always ready to offer tailored solutions, insightful advice, and steadfast support, ensuring that your business is well-positioned to seize opportunities and overcome any obstacles in the dynamic world of international trade. With SL3 Consulting, you gain a service provider and a partner committed to your success. A Trade Finance Standby Letter of Credit (SBLC)

A Standby Letter of Credit (SBLC) is a financial instrument frequently used in international trade to provide security and assurance for both buyers and sellers. Issued by a bank on behalf of its client, usually the buyer, the SBLC guarantees that the client will fulfill their payment obligations to the seller. This tool acts as a safety net for the beneficiary by ensuring payment if the party requesting the letter (the applicant) fails to meet their contractual duties. The SBLC is particularly valuable in situations where the financial reliability of a party is in question.

For instance, in international trade, a seller from one country might require an SBLC from a buyer in another to secure the assurance that payment will be received. This serves as a sign of good faith and demonstrates the buyer's financial credibility.

To secure an SBLC, the applicant must approach a bank, which will likely require collateral or a cash deposit. The bank then evaluates the applicant's creditworthiness before issuing the SBLC, which functions as a contingent obligation—activated only if the applicant defaults on payment. While not intended as the primary payment method, the SBLC is a crucial backup.

Should the buyer fail to meet the payment terms, the seller can present the SBLC to the issuing bank as a claim for payment. Upon validating the claim, the bank compensates the seller for the amount specified in the SBLC. This instrument is versatile, used across various transactions, including real estate, construction projects, and international commerce, and is particularly beneficial when dealing with unfamiliar or overseas partners.

The primary advantage of an SBLC is its role in reducing transaction risk for the seller by offering a payment guarantee. For buyers, securing contracts or procuring goods and services is an effective mechanism, especially without a strong relationship with the seller. Ultimately, the Standby Letter of Credit is pivotal in mitigating payment risks in business transactions and enhancing trust and confidence in high-value and cross-border dealings.

International Project Financing

Trade Finance International Project Funding is a specialized financial mechanism to support global trade ventures and projects. It facilitates cross-border transactions by providing essential funding and risk mitigation services to exporters, importers, and other participants involved in global trade.

Performance Bond

A trade finance performance bond, or a performance guarantee, is a financial instrument to ensure that a seller fulfills their contractual obligations as agreed upon with the buyer. Typically used in construction projects and other large-scale contracts, a performance bond acts as a financial guarantee that a contractor will complete a project according to the specified quality, timeline, and specifications.

If a contractor fails to meet these obligations, the project owner can file a claim against the bond. The surety company issuing the bond has several options: it can provide financial support to the original contractor to complete the project, appoint a new contractor, or compensate the project owner for the financial loss up to the bond's value. Performance bonds are crucial in the construction industry, especially for public or large-scale private projects, as they provide insurance that the project will be completed per the contractual agreement.

Bank Guarantees

A Trade Finance Bank Guarantee (BG) is a financial instrument issued by a bank to ensure payment to a third party in a trade transaction on behalf of its client. It acts as a secure commitment from the bank to fulfill the client's financial obligations if they cannot do so themselves. This guarantee provides security to the beneficiary, typically the seller or supplier, ensuring they receive payment for goods or services rendered, even if the buyer defaults.

Bank guarantees are particularly valuable in international trade, where the distance and differing legal systems between parties can increase the risk of non-payment. When a company engages in a transaction, especially internationally, the seller may require a guarantee that they will receive payment once they deliver the goods or services. The buyer's bank issues this guarantee, assuring the seller of payment up to a specified amount. This shifts the risk of non-payment from the seller to the bank, mitigating potential concerns about the buyer's creditworthiness or complexities of international trade laws.

Trade Finance Bank Guarantees are widely utilized in various international transactions, including purchasing goods and services and bidding in international tenders. They are essential in deals involving high-value transactions or when dealing with new trading partners, forming part of a broader category of trade finance tools that address the risks associated with cross-border trade.

Bid/ Tender Bond

Trade finance bid tender bond, commonly referred to as a bid bond or tender bond, is a financial instrument issued by a bank or a surety company on behalf of a contractor or bidder in response to a request for proposal (RFP) or tender issued by a project owner or government entity. The primary function of the bid tender bond is to assure the project owner that the bidder is serious and committed to executing the contractual obligations if their bid is successful and they are awarded the project.

This bond is a financial guarantee in the tendering process, mainly prevalent in the construction industry and other large-scale project bids. It ensures the project owner that the bidder (contractor) will honor their bid and undertake the project if awarded the contract. The bond deters bidders from withdrawing their bids prematurely or failing to initiate the contract at their proposed price upon winning the bid.

The procedure begins when a bidder submits a bid accompanied by a bank or surety company tender bond. This bond typically represents a percentage of the bid amount, signifying to the project owner the bidder's serious intent and financial capacity to manage the project. The bond is forfeited if the bidder is selected but subsequently declines to proceed. The project owner may then claim the bond amount as compensation for securing another contractor and any potential increase in project costs.

Tender bonds play a vital role in large projects involving multiple bidders by ensuring that only serious and capable bidders participate in the tendering process. This is especially crucial when the cost of preparing bids is substantial, and project owners seek to minimize the risk of project delays or cancellations due to bidders retracting their offers.

A tender bond is an essential financial tool in the tendering process. It gives project owners financial security and confidence that the bidders are committed to their proposals, facilitating a more efficient and dependable bidding process.

International Real Estate Investments

International real estate investments involve acquiring, owning, or developing properties outside an investor's home country. These investments provide opportunities for diversification, capital growth, and potential income generation in foreign markets. Investors might opt for various properties, including residential, commercial, industrial, or mixed-use developments.

Documentary Letter of Credit

A Documentary Letter of Credit, also known as a commercial letter of credit or documentary credit, is a predominant payment method in international trade. Issued by a bank at the buyer's request (the applicant), it guarantees payment to the seller (the beneficiary) under the contract terms, typically after the seller ships the goods to the buyer. This financial instrument is crucial in international transactions where the buyer and seller may be unfamiliar with each other's legal systems and where trust levels might be low.

The process starts when the buyer and seller agree to use a letter of credit as the payment method in their contract. The buyer applies for a letter of credit from their bank, which assesses the buyer's creditworthiness before issuance. Once issued, the letter of credit is forwarded to the seller's bank, which notifies the seller. Upon shipping the goods, the seller presents the required shipping documents to their bank, which forwards them to the buyer's bank. Suppose the documents comply with all the conditions of the letter of credit. In that case, the issuing bank releases the funds to the seller.

For the seller, a documentary letter of credit offers a guaranteed payment from a reputable bank, mitigating the risk of non-payment. For the buyer, it ensures that they are only obliged to pay once the goods have been shipped as per the agreement. Additionally, a letter of credit can smooth trade negotiations by providing a clear, agreed-upon framework for the conditions under which payment will be released.

Overall, the documentary letter of credit is an indispensable tool in international commerce, providing a secure mechanism that carefully balances the needs and risks of both parties involved in cross-border trade.

RWA/POF Documents

RWA (Ready, Willing, and Able)

RWA is an official declaration provided by a bank or financial institution on behalf of a buyer, affirming their readiness, willingness, and financial ability to proceed with a specific trade transaction. This statement demonstrates the buyer's intent and capability to fulfill the obligations stipulated in the contract.

POF (Proof of Funds)

POF is a certification or statement from a bank or financial institution verifying that a buyer has the necessary funds to complete a trade deal. Sellers often require this proof to ensure the buyer has the financial resources to conclude the transaction successfully.

Real Estate Lending at SL3 Consulting

At SL3 Consulting, we streamline the borrowing process to enhance efficiency and ensure timely deal closures. The speed of closing transactions primarily depends on the cooperation of the borrower or broker. Typically, we can close transactions within 7 to 10 business days, assuming all required documentation is promptly submitted.

Process Overview

1. **Initial Contact:** The process starts with an initial call or email to evaluate the feasibility of the loan request, which is crucial for understanding the borrower's specific needs.

2. **Application Submission:** The borrower or broker submits a loan application following the initial assessment.

3. **Issuance of Term Sheet:** A Loan Officer reviews the application and issues a term sheet detailing the loan terms.

4. **Signing of Term Sheet:** The process formally begins once the borrower or broker signs and returns the term sheet.

5. **Document Submission:** The borrower or broker must then provide a complete package of documents required for

the loan.

6. **Underwriting Review:** Our underwriting team thoroughly reviews all submitted documents.

7. **Clarification Requests:** If necessary, the underwriting team may request additional information for clarification.

8. **Submission of Additional Information:** The borrower responds with any requested information for clarification.

9. **Closing Phase:** The transaction moves to the closing phase once all documentation is complete and clarifications are addressed.

10. Completion: The deal is finalized and considered successfully closed.

This structured approach ensures each step is efficiently managed, leading to a smooth and expedient lending process.

Borrower Experience Requirements

Investment Experience and Financing Options

No prior investment experience is necessary for new borrowers at SL3 Consulting, as we offer financing options tailored for newcomers. However, to qualify for maximum leverage, a borrower should have a history of purchasing at least three investment properties in the past three years. Alternatively, three years of experience as a contractor, property manager, or real estate agent may qualify a borrower for higher leverage.

Credit Criteria

SL3 Consulting does not impose a minimum credit score requirement for borrowers. However, individuals with a credit score below 550 must make interest reserve payments as part of their loan terms.

Immediate Disqualifiers

Specific conditions may prevent a borrower from qualifying for a loan with us. These conditions are evaluated with careful consideration, as each case is unique. Disqualifying factors include:

- A bankruptcy filed within the last four years, with each case examined on its own merits to assess the nuances of the situation.

- A foreclosure within the previous four years approached with a detailed, case-by-case analysis.

- Any history of short sales or deeds instead of foreclosure within the past four years, individually evaluated to understand the context and implications.

- A record of any financial crimes or fraud is a critical factor in our evaluation process that directly impacts the integrity and security of the lending process.

Our approach to these conditions is rooted in a thorough and individualized review, ensuring a fair and comprehensive assessment of each applicant's financial history.

Broker and Referral Program

SL3 Consulting collaborates with industry professionals who are dedicated to helping customers secure better financing solutions. Our team comprises experts across various fields, ensuring your clients benefit from tailored products. SL3 Consulting Brokers are part of a collaborative team that values autonomy and the business you bring. Our process is designed to be smooth and simple, allowing brokers to continue to outpace the competition by freeing up their time to scout for new deals and clients. Simply submit an application from your client, and we handle the rest, aiming to close real estate deals within 5-21 days. Once a deal closes, you get compensated directly for the transaction and can continue your search.

Additionally, we are SBA-approved to offer the 7(a) and 504 programs aimed at assisting you in better understanding the markets you work with. From bridge loans and business acquisition financing to hard money loans and commercial real estate loans, along with private equity lenders, VC firms, and investors. We also offer unsecured business lines of credit for those with more non-traditional financial needs.

Our Ethical Values

At SL3 Consulting, we deeply value the trust our customers place in us, viewing it as the foundation of our business. Our commitment to ethical practices is steadfast, ensuring that every decision we make adheres to the highest standards of integrity. This dedication to ethical conduct establishes our platform as a bastion of trust and morality within the investment community.

Innovation with Ethical Intent

Our approach to innovation is driven by purpose. We do not innovate merely for novelty; every new feature or service we introduce is thoughtfully designed to further our mission of promoting ethical, transparent, and accessible investing and deal-making. True innovation must align with our core values and contribute positively to our users and the broader investment community.

Empowerment through Education

We staunchly believe in the power of knowledge. Education is a transformative tool, and we are committed to equipping our users with comprehensive resources. We aim to empower them to make well-informed, impactful, and beneficial decisions. This commitment to education ensures that our users are not merely participants in the investment world but informed actors capable of making significant contributions.

Commitment to Transparent Transactions

Transparency is a fundamental principle of our operations. We strive to ensure that every transaction, process, and outcome is clear and comprehensible to our users. This transparency is crucial in building and maintaining trust, ensuring our users can confidently engage with our platform's integrity and openness.

Global Vision with a Personal Approach

While SL3 Consulting operates globally, our service approach is intensely personal. We recognize and value the uniqueness of each community member, striving to ensure that every interaction is meaningful and tailored to individual needs and circumstances. This blend of a broad vision and personal touch allows us to connect more effectively with our diverse clientele.

Celebrating Diversity

The strength of SL3 Consulting lies in the diversity of our community, which includes a broad spectrum of investors, visionaries, and team members. We celebrate and embrace this diversity, understanding that it enriches our platform and expands our perspectives. This diversity fosters a more inclusive, innovative, and comprehensive approach to investment and business, reflecting various viewpoints and experiences. In summary, SL3 Consulting maintains an ethical, educational, transparent, and personalized platform while celebrating the diversity that strengthens and distinguishes our community.

Broker and Referral Program

At SL3 Consulting, we take great pride in collaborating with industry professionals who are dedicated to helping customers secure superior financing solutions. Our team comprises experts across various fields, ensuring that each client benefits from the confidence of customized financial products. Our brokers, integral members of our collaborative team, are highly valued for their independence and the significant business opportunities they contribute.

Our process is meticulously crafted to provide our brokers a streamlined and seamless experience. This essential efficiency enables them to maintain a competitive edge by freeing valuable time to pursue new deals and clients. The simplicity of our process allows brokers to simply submit a client application to us; we take care of everything else, ensuring the deal is funded efficiently. Our dedicated staff is committed to swiftly closing your real estate deals, typically within 5 to 21 days. Upon the completion of a deal, brokers receive their payment directly from the HUD, allowing them to immediately continue their search for new opportunities.

We are also proud to be an SBA-approved entity, offering the 7(a) and 504 loan programs. We aim to enhance your understanding of your markets by providing various financing options. These include bridge loans, business acquisition financing, hard money loans, commercial real estate loans, and funding from private equity lenders and venture capital firms. We also cater to clients with unconventional financial needs by offering unsecured business lines of credit.

Our diverse array of financing solutions is designed to meet the varied needs of our clients, whether they are engaged in traditional or non-traditional financial ventures. At SL3 Consulting, we are committed to supporting our brokers and clients with a comprehensive understanding of the market, a broad range of financing options, and an efficient and effective process.

Private Equity In Real Estate

Private equity in real estate refers to investment funds or companies using pooled capital from accredited investors to directly acquire real estate properties. This investment can take several forms, each with its advantages and challenges.

Private Equity Real Estate Joint Ventures

Joint ventures represent a strategic approach in the real estate sector, where private equity firms collaborate with other investors or developers to pool resources, share risks, and leverage collective expertise. This collaborative model is particularly prevalent in large-scale projects, including developing rental properties with substantial stakes and capital requirements.

Advantages of Joint Ventures

One of the primary advantages of joint ventures is the distribution of risk. By sharing the financial burden among several parties, each participant can mitigate their individual exposure to potential losses. This is particularly attractive in volatile markets or projects with unpredictable outcomes, such as new developments in emerging areas. Additionally, joint ventures allow participants to undertake larger projects than they might be able to manage independently, potentially leading to higher returns.

Furthermore, joint ventures provide access to a broader range of expertise. For example, a private equity firm with significant capital but limited local market knowledge might partner with a regional developer who understands the local real estate environment but lacks the necessary funds to single-handedly execute a project. This combination can enhance the project's success rate. An example is the partnership between private equity giant Blackstone and local real estate companies to develop large-scale rental properties in various global markets. Such collaborations combine Blackstone's financial muscle with local firms' operational expertise, optimizing the management of rental properties to maximize occupancy rates and rental yields.

Challenges and Risks

However, the joint venture model is not without challenges. The need for detailed agreements can lead to complexity in structuring deals. To prevent disputes, these agreements must carefully delineate each party's roles, contributions, and profit-sharing arrangements. They must also consider exit strategies and conflict resolution mechanisms critical to the partnership's long-term success.

Moreover, joint ventures can be prone to management conflicts, especially if the partners have differing business cultures, management styles, or visions for the project. For instance, disputes might arise regarding decisions on property management, tenant selection, or reinvestment versus distribution of profits. Such conflicts, if not resolved amicably, can jeopardize the entire project.

An illustrative case is a joint venture between Tishman Speyer and Lehman Brothers in 2007 to purchase and operate Archstone, a large portfolio of rental properties. The partnership faced challenges during the financial crisis, with disagreements on management and financial strategies contributing to strain on the venture. Ultimately, these conflicts, combined with market downturns, led to substantial financial losses and complicated the unwinding of the partnership.

While joint ventures in real estate offer the potential for reduced risk and access to additional expertise, they require robust, clear agreements and effective conflict resolution strategies to be successful. These collaborations can lead to significant rewards, such as the successful development and operation of rental properties. Still, they demand careful planning, strong partnership relations, and proactive management to navigate the inherent complexities of joint investment undertakings. Investors considering joint ventures must evaluate these factors to ensure the alignment of goals and the smooth execution of real estate projects.

Here is an example of a small Duplex Real Estate business owner seeking Financing from a Private Equity investor.

A workflow for a small duplex owner seeking funding from a private equity partner through a joint venture strategy involves several critical steps, from the initial planning and proposal stage to the final agreement and ongoing management. A detailed workflow:

Initial Assessment and Preparation

- Property Evaluation: Assess the duplex's value, revenue-generating potential, and any improvements needed.
- Market Analysis: Study market trends, rental demand, and comparable properties to understand potential ROI.
- Objective Setting: Define clear objectives for the joint venture, including financial goals and timelines.

Identifying Potential Partners

- Research Potential Partners: Identify private equity firms or individual investors interested in real estate ventures.
- Initial Contact: Reach out to potential partners through networking, industry events, or direct outreach.

- Preliminary Discussions: Share basic property and market information to gauge interest.

Proposal Development

- Detailed Proposal Creation: Develop a comprehensive investment proposal that includes financial projections, market analysis, and details about the property.
- Business Plan: Outline the business strategy for managing and capitalizing on the duplex, including proposed renovations, marketing for tenants, and financial management.

Negotiation and Agreement Formation

- Initial Meetings: Conduct meetings to discuss the proposal in detail, clarify objectives, and negotiate terms.
- Due Diligence: Allow the potential partner to perform due diligence to verify the property's potential and financial assumptions.
- Agreement Drafting: Draft a joint venture agreement that details roles, contributions, profit sharing, management responsibilities, and dispute resolution mechanisms.

Legal Review and Finalization

- Legal Consultation: Consult legal professionals to ensure the agreement complies with local real estate laws and partnership regulations.

- Final Negotiations: Make any necessary adjustments to the agreement based on legal advice and partner feedback.
- Signing: Both parties sign the joint venture agreement, formalizing the partnership.

Capital Injection and Project Initiation

- Funding: The private equity partner provides the agreed-upon capital.
- Project Execution: Begin any renovations or improvements as planned. Implement the business strategy for property management.

Operational Management and Reporting

- Management Activities: Manage the duplex according to the joint venture agreement. This includes tenant management, maintenance, and financial management.
- Regular Reporting: Provide the partner with regular financial and operational reports as agreed in the joint venture terms.
- Ongoing Communication: Maintain open lines of communication with the partner to discuss any issues or opportunities.

Review and Exit Strategy

- Performance Review: Periodically review the investment's performance against the set objectives.
- Exit Planning: Depending on the agreement's terms,

plan for the eventual exit of the partnership, which might include selling the property or buying out the partner's share.

This ensures that the duplex owner and the private equity partner are clear about their roles and expectations, leading to a more successful joint venture. Proper planning, transparency, and legal safeguards are key to mitigating risks and maximizing the potential benefits of the partnership.

Direct Acquisitions

Direct acquisitions in real estate through private equity involve firms using investor funds to purchase properties outright, encompassing control and flexibility over property management and the potential for high returns. These acquisitions come with their own set of advantages and challenges that are crucial for investors to understand.

Advantages of Direct Acquisitions

One of the primary advantages of direct acquisitions is the control and flexibility it grants over property management. Private equity firms can select properties based on their potential, manage them directly, and decide on the timing and manner of their sale. This level of control allows firms to implement value-enhancing strategies, such as renovating a property or improving its tenant mix, which can lead to substantial increases in property value. For instance, The Blackstone Group has demonstrated the potential of this approach with numerous successful real estate investments, including the transformative acquisition and management of Hilton Worldwide.

Furthermore, direct acquisitions often lead to high potential returns. By making strategic improvements and optimizing the management of their properties, firms can significantly increase the value of their investments. These returns are generally higher than those from more passive real estate investments, reflecting the added risk and effort involved in direct management.

Challenges of Direct Acquisitions

However, direct acquisitions are not without their challenges. One significant barrier is the substantial capital requirement, which restricts participation to investors who can afford to commit large sums of money. This high entry barrier means direct acquisitions are often out of reach for smaller investors.

Moreover, these investments are highly susceptible to market fluctuations. Real estate markets can experience rapid changes due to economic shifts, regulatory changes, or other external factors. Such volatility can adversely affect property values, as seen during the 2008 financial crisis when many real estate investments plummeted.

Each property has specific risks, including tenant issues, maintenance demands, and local market changes. For example, the acquisition of Stuyvesant Town–Peter Cooper Village in New York by a consortium led by Tishman Speyer became infamous for its failure. The consortium's plan to convert rent-stabilized apartments into luxury units was thwarted by legal and market challenges, leading to a financial debacle.

Direct acquisitions in real estate through private equity can offer significant advantages in management control and the potential for high returns; they also require substantial capital and expose investors to market fluctuations and property-specific risks. Such investments demand a deep understanding of market dynamics and skilled property management, highlighting the need for expertise and strategic planning in navigating these complex investments.

Real Estate Funds

Real estate funds managed by private equity firms allow investors to pool their capital into a collective investment vehicle that acquires a diversified portfolio of properties. This approach blends professional management with the advantages of diversification. Still, it also comes with inherent drawbacks related to liquidity and cost.

Advantages of Real Estate Funds

The primary advantage of investing in real estate funds is diversification. Investing in various properties across different geographic locations and market segments (such as residential, commercial, and industrial) significantly reduces the risk associated with any single investment. For example, a commercial real estate market downturn might be offset by stable returns in residential real estate within the same fund, stabilizing overall fund performance.

Moreover, these funds are managed by professional

managers with the expertise and resources to identify opportunities, manage properties, and execute exit strategies. This professional management can potentially lead to higher returns than individual investors might achieve. A notable example of successful real estate fund management is the TIAA Real Estate Account, which has consistently provided competitive returns to its investors by strategically acquiring high-quality properties and managing them effectively.

Challenges of Real Estate Funds

Real estate funds are not without their challenges. One significant drawback is limited liquidity. Unlike stocks, real estate is not a liquid asset, and funds typically lock in capital for five to ten years to allow time for property acquisition, management, and disposal. This lock-up period can be a major disadvantage for investors who need access to their capital or prefer more liquid investments.

Additionally, the costs associated with managing these funds can be substantial. Management fees and performance fees can diminish net returns to investors. These fees are usually a percentage of assets under management or a percentage of the profits earned by the fund, respectively. For instance, it's common for funds to charge a 1-2% management fee annually on managed assets and a 20% performance fee on profits, which can significantly reduce the effective return to investors.

In summary, while real estate funds offer diversification and professional management that can enhance returns, investors must weigh these benefits against the limitations of limited liquidity and the impact of fees on overall investment returns. Each investor's decision to invest in a real estate fund should consider these factors along with their financial goals, investment horizon, and risk tolerance.

Real Estate Investment Trusts (REITs) offer a distinctive avenue for investment in real estate, combining elements of income stability with the growth potential of real estate markets. Managed by private equity firms or specialized management companies, REITs provide an accessible and structured method for investing in a diversified portfolio of real estate assets.

Benefits of Investing in REITs

A key characteristic of REITs is their requirement to distribute at least 90% of their taxable income to shareholders as dividends, which ensures a consistent and regular income stream for investors. This makes REITs particularly attractive for income-focused investors. Additionally, REITs receive favorable tax treatment because they are generally exempt from corporate income tax at the federal level, provided they meet certain regulatory requirements. This tax efficiency can potentially enhance the returns available to investors.

For example, Equity Residential, a large publicly traded REIT specializing in residential properties, has consistently provided strong dividend yields to its investors, demonstrating the potential for REITs to deliver regular income alongside capital appreciation.

Challenges and Risks Associated with REITs

Despite these advantages, REITs face a range of challenges and risks. One of the primary challenges is the significant regulatory and compliance costs associated with maintaining REIT status. These entities must comply with complex regulations regarding income distribution, asset composition, and transparency. Failure to meet these standards can result in loss of tax-advantaged status, significantly affecting profitability and investor returns.

REITs are subject to market risks. Factors such as economic downturns, changes in interest rates, and fluctuations in property values can impact the performance of a REIT. For instance, during the financial crisis 2008, many REITs saw substantial declines in their asset values and dividend payouts, reflecting the turmoil in the real estate markets.

An illustrative example of this risk was the case of General Growth Properties (GGP), one of the largest mall operators in the United States, which filed for bankruptcy in 2009 due to its inability to refinance its debt amidst the credit crunch.

REITs offer several benefits, including regular income distributions and tax advantages; they also require careful consideration of the associated regulatory burdens and exposure to real estate market dynamics. Potential investors should weigh these factors carefully against their investment objectives and risk tolerance. The ability of REITs to provide income and growth makes them a unique component of the real estate investment landscape, suitable for a broad range of investment strategies.

Real Estate Debt Investing

Real estate debt investing presents an alternative strategy for private equity firms, focusing on income generation through interest payments rather than direct equity stakes in properties. This method involves investing in the debt associated with real estate, such as mortgages or construction loans. The appeal of this approach lies in its capacity to provide steady income and inherent security. Still, it carries distinct risks and yields lower returns than equity investments.

Advantages of Real Estate Debt Investing

The primary advantage of investing in real estate debt is the steady income generated from interest payments. Investors benefit from predictable returns based on fixed or floating interest rates tied to the loans. This regular income can be particularly attractive when steady cash flow is a priority during volatile market conditions.

Moreover, the property generally secures these debt investments, offering protection not typically available in equity investments. In the event of a borrower default, the lender (investor) has the right to seize the property to recover the owed funds. This security feature reduces the overall risk of the investment, making it appealing to conservative investors.

An example of successful real estate debt investing can

be seen in the approach taken by large investment firms like Blackstone. They have diversified their investments to include significant positions in real estate debt, capitalizing on these instruments' protective features and steady returns, particularly in uncertain economic times.

Challenges and Risks of Real Estate Debt Investing

Despite its advantages, real estate debt investing is not without its challenges. The primary risk involved is credit risk—the possibility that the borrower will fail to meet the loan terms. While the property secures the loan, defaults can still lead to financial loss, especially if the property value has declined or selling the property does not cover the loan balance. Foreclosing and selling a property can be lengthy and costly, potentially eroding the returns from interest payments.

Additionally, real estate debt investments generally offer lower returns than equity investments. This is due to their lower risk profile; since lenders are prioritized over equity investors in the event of a liquidation, the potential upside in rising markets is also limited. For instance, during a real estate boom, equity holders might see significant appreciation in property values and corresponding increases in profit. In contrast, debt holders would only receive their fixed interest payments.

Furthermore, market conditions such as interest rate changes can affect the attractiveness of real estate debt investments. Rising interest rates can reduce the value of fixed-rate debt instruments, making them less profitable than new market issues. This scenario was observed during periods of monetary tightening by central banks, where existing bonds with lower rates become less valuable.

Real estate debt investing offers a more secure and stable investment option within the real estate sector, ideal for those seeking regular income and lower-risk exposure. However, the trade-off for this security is lower potential returns and exposure to credit and market risks. Private equity firms engaging in this type of investment must carefully assess the creditworthiness of borrowers and the potential impact of market fluctuations on their investment portfolios. Thus, while real estate debt can be a valuable part of a diversified investment strategy, it requires meticulous management to navigate its inherent complexities effectively.

How I Became a Private Equity Broker

My journey to becoming a private equity broker began with understanding finance. I immersed myself in understanding the fundamentals of business and economics, knowing this solid foundation was crucial. Recognizing the competitive nature of the industry, I also earned several certifications programs.

With my educational background solidified, I started my career in finance by launching my own financial firm. These roles were critical for understanding the industry and developing essential skills. I didn't just stick to my desk; I actively attended industry events and engaged with professionals, steadily building a network of contacts.

As I gained experience, I focused on honing my analytical skills, learning to assess financial systems and market trends in real estate with precision. I worked diligently on improving my communication skills, practicing how to present investment ideas clearly and persuasively. Negotiation, a key part of closing deals, became another area of expertise for me as I learned the art of striking the best terms for my clients.

Participating in successful investment deals was a turning point for me. I meticulously documented my achievements, showcasing my ability to generate significant returns for investors. This track record became a powerful tool in attracting future investors and building my reputation in the industry.

Understanding the regulatory landscape was essential, so I familiarized myself with securities laws like the Securities Act of 1933 and the Securities Exchange Act of 1934. I ensured compliance with all relevant regulations, including Anti-Money Laundering (AML) and Know Your Customer (KYC) rules, to avoid any legal pitfalls.

Depending on my location, I knew I might need to register as a broker-dealer with the Securities and Exchange Commission (SEC) or obtain state licenses. I navigated these requirements meticulously, ensuring I was always operating within legal boundaries.

Building relationships with high-net-worth individuals, institutional investors, and family offices became a priority. I attended industry events and expanded my network, forming strategic partnerships with financial institutions and advisory firms to access more resources and investor pools.

Crafting well-researched investment proposals was another area where I excelled. I clearly outlined potential returns, risks, and exit strategies, tailoring each proposal to meet the preferences of my target investors. Transparency was key—I was always upfront about fees, terms, and conditions, and provided regular updates on investment progress to maintain investor confidence.

Leveraging technology played a significant role in my success. I used online platforms, social media, and digital marketing strategies to reach a wider audience of potential investors. Technology helped me manage relationships and promote investment opportunities efficiently.

Throughout my journey, I maintained high ethical standards and avoided conflicts of interest. My integrity-built trust with both investors and regulators, cementing my reputation as a reliable and honest broker.

I never stopped learning. I stayed updated on market trends, new regulations, and industry best practices. Continuous professional development allowed me to adapt to changes and seize new opportunities, ensuring a rewarding and successful career in finance.

Through hard work, dedication, and an unwavering commitment to excellence, I became a respected private equity broker, creating significant value for my investors and achieving my career aspirations.

How to raise capital

Raising capital as a private equity broker involves building strong relationships with investors, showcasing successful deals, and demonstrating expertise in finding profitable investment opportunities. Networking within the financial community and presenting attractive investment opportunities are essential. Staying updated on market trends and regulatory requirements is also crucial.

If you're raising capital through methods like loan agreements or revenue-sharing, you typically don't need to file forms with the Securities and Exchange Commission (SEC). However, if your activities involve investments considered securities under U.S. law, you may need to comply with securities regulations and file forms with the

SEC.

For example, if your investment opportunity qualifies as a security under the Securities Act of 1933, you might need to file Form D with the SEC for private placements exempt from registration under Regulation D. Form D provides the SEC with basic information about the offering and parties involved.

If your fundraising doesn't involve securities, you generally don't need to file forms with the SEC. Instead, focus on complying with other laws and regulations, such as anti-fraud laws and business regulations.

Evaluate your fundraising activities carefully and consult legal professionals to determine if securities laws apply. They can help you navigate compliance requirements and the regulatory landscape.

1. Develop a Solid Network: Build relationships with high-net-worth individuals, institutional investors, family offices, and other capital sources. Attend industry events, conferences, and networking functions to expand your network.

2. Demonstrate Expertise: Show your industry knowledge and expertise in specific sectors or investment strategies. Investors trust people who understand the markets they operate in.

3. Create Compelling Investment Proposals: Prepare well-researched proposals that clearly outline potential returns, risks, and exit strategies. Tailor these proposals to match the preferences and objectives of your target

investors.

4. Provide Transparency: Build trust by being transparent about fees, terms, and conditions. Provide regular updates on investment progress.

5. Build a Track Record: Highlight a history of successful deals to show your ability to generate returns. Showcase past successes and the value you've created for clients.

6. Stay Compliant: Ensure your fundraising activities comply with relevant regulations and legal requirements. Familiarize yourself with securities laws governing private placements to avoid legal issues.

7. Leverage Technology: Use technology to streamline fundraising and reach more potential investors. Utilize online platforms, social media, and digital marketing to promote investment opportunities.

8. Seek Strategic Partnerships: Partner with financial institutions, advisory firms, or industry experts to leverage their networks and resources. Strategic partnerships can help access new investors and enhance credibility.

By following these steps and consistently delivering value to investors, you can effectively raise capital as a private equity broker.

There are legal considerations and regulations that you need to adhere to when raising capital as a private equity broker. They include:

1. Securities Laws: Follow securities laws like the Securities Act of 1933 and the Securities Exchange Act of 1934. These laws regulate the offer and sale of securities and

require SEC registration unless exemptions apply.

2. Regulatory Filings: Depending on the type of offering and jurisdiction, you may need to file documents with regulatory authorities, such as Form D with the SEC for private placements or comply with state Blue Sky Laws.

3. Disclosure Requirements: Provide investors with complete and accurate information about the investment, including risks, fees, and conflicts of interest. Inadequate disclosures can lead to legal issues.

4. AML and KYC Regulations: Implement Anti-Money Laundering (AML) and Know Your Customer (KYC) procedures to prevent money laundering and verify investor identities.

5. Licensing and Registration: Private equity brokers may need to be licensed or registered with regulatory bodies, such as the SEC or state agencies.

6. Ethical Standards: Maintain ethical standards and avoid conflicts of interest. Adhere to industry codes of conduct to build and keep trust with investors and regulators.

It's important to consult with legal professionals specializing in securities law and regulatory compliance to ensure your fundraising activities comply with all applicable laws and regulations. Violating securities laws can result in severe legal and financial consequences, so it's crucial to prioritize compliance in your capital-raising efforts.

Why Join SL3 Consulting?

If you're looking for a rewarding career in financial markets, I believe private equity brokerage offers some of the most lucrative opportunities available. At my firm, we provide the resources and support you need to launch a successful career with us.

At our firm, we value education and professional development. We support your pursuit of advanced degrees and certifications such as the MBA and Chartered Financial Analyst (CFA) designation. This commitment to education ensures that our brokers are among the most knowledgeable and skilled in the industry.

Starting your career with us means gaining invaluable experience in entry-level positions in investment banking, financial analysis, and consulting. These roles will help you understand the intricacies of the financial industry and develop essential skills. Additionally, we encourage our brokers to actively attend industry events and engage with professionals on platforms like LinkedIn. By joining our firm, you'll expand your network significantly, opening doors to potential clients and valuable industry contacts.

Our firm is dedicated to helping you hone critical skills. You'll learn to analyze financial statements and market trends with precision, present investment ideas persuasively, and negotiate deals effectively. We believe in continuous improvement and provide the resources to help you excel. Joining our team means becoming part of a firm with a strong track record of successful deals. We meticulously document our achievements, showcasing our ability to generate significant returns for investors. This proven success attracts future investors and builds your reputation as a reliable broker.

We ensure that our brokers are well-versed in securities laws and compliance requirements, including Anti-Money Laundering (AML) and Know Your Customer (KYC) rules. Our firm provides the guidance and training needed to navigate the regulatory landscape effectively. Depending on your location, we help you register as a broker-dealer with the Securities and Exchange Commission (SEC) or obtain necessary state licenses. We handle these complexities, allowing you to focus on building your career.

We have established relationships with high-net-worth individuals, institutional investors, and family offices. By joining us, you'll benefit from our extensive network and form strategic partnerships with financial institutions and advisory firms, giving you access to more resources and investor pools. Our firm excels at crafting well-researched investment proposals that clearly outline potential returns, risks, and exit strategies. We prioritize transparency, ensuring that all fees, terms, and conditions are communicated upfront. Regular updates on investment progress build and maintain investor confidence.

We use the latest technology to enhance our fundraising efforts and reach a wider audience of potential investors. Our online platforms, social media presence, and digital marketing strategies help you manage relationships and promote investment opportunities efficiently. Integrity and professionalism are at the core of our firm's values. We maintain high ethical standards and avoid conflicts of interest, building trust with investors and regulators alike.

The financial landscape is constantly evolving, and we ensure our brokers stay updated on market trends, new regulations, and industry best practices. We support continuous professional development, enabling you to adapt and seize new opportunities. By joining our private equity firm, you'll be part of a team dedicated to excellence, continuous learning, and ethical conduct.

We provide the resources, support, and opportunities needed to build a successful and fulfilling career in private equity brokerage. Take the next step with us and realize your full potential in the financial markets.

How to Determine Your Net worth

Net Worth Calculation Worksheet

Instructions

Use this worksheet to calculate your net worth by listing all your assets and liabilities. Net worth is calculated by subtracting your total liabilities from your total assets. This worksheet will help you understand your financial situation and track your progress.

Assets

1. Cash and Cash Equivalents:
    - Savings Account:
    - Checking Account:
    - Cash on Hand:
    - Total Cash and Cash Equivalents:
2. Investments:
    - Stocks:
    - Bonds:
    - Mutual Funds:
    - Retirement Accounts (e.g., 401(k), IRA):
    - Other Investments (e.g., real estate, cryptocurrency):
    - Total Investments:
3. Real Estate:
    - Primary Residence:
    - Rental Properties:
    - Other Real Estate Holdings:
    - Total Real Estate:
4. Personal Property:

- Vehicles:
- Jewelry:
- Electronics:
- Furniture and Appliances:
- Other Personal Property:
- Total Personal Property:

5. Other Assets:
   - Business Ownership:
   - Collectibles:
   - Other Assets:
   - Total Other Assets:

Total Assets: _______________________________________

Liabilities

1. Mortgage(s):
   - Primary Residence:
   - Rental Properties:
   - Other Mortgages:
   - Total Mortgage Debt:

2. Consumer Debt:
   - Credit Card Debt:
   - Personal Loans:
   - Student Loans:
   - Auto Loans:
   - Other Consumer Debt:
   - Total Consumer Debt:

3. Other Liabilities:
   - Business Loans:
   - Tax Debt:
   - Other Liabilities:
   - Total Other Liabilities:

Total Liabilities: _______________________________

Net Worth Calculation

Total Assets - Total Liabilities = Net Worth
Net Worth = Total Assets - Total Liabilities